50 Bangkok Nights Recipes

By: Kelly Johnson

Table of Contents

- Pad Thai
- Tom Yum Goong (Spicy Shrimp Soup)
- Green Curry (Gaeng Keow Wan)
- Massaman Curry
- Tom Kha Gai (Chicken Coconut Soup)
- Som Tum (Green Papaya Salad)
- Larb Gai (Spicy Chicken Salad)
- Pad Kra Pao (Basil Chicken)
- Pad See Ew (Stir-Fried Flat Noodles)
- Khao Pad (Thai Fried Rice)
- Moo Pad Krapow (Stir-Fried Pork with Basil)
- Pla Rad Prik (Crispy Fish with Chili Sauce)
- Gai Yang (Grilled Chicken)
- Thai Fish Cakes (Tod Mun Pla)
- Thai Beef Salad (Yum Nua)
- Khao Soi (Curry Noodle Soup)
- Thai Spring Rolls
- Thai Chili and Garlic Noodles
- Thai Grilled Pork Skewers (Moo Ping)
- Green Mango Salad
- Thai Fried Tofu with Peanut Sauce
- Pad Woon Sen (Stir-Fried Glass Noodles)
- Thai Pineapple Fried Rice
- Thai Vegetable Stir-Fry (Pad Pak Ruam Mit)
- Spicy Glass Noodle Salad (Yum Woon Sen)
- Thai Garlic Pepper Chicken
- Thai Red Curry with Duck
- Thai Spicy Seafood Salad (Yum Talay)
- Thai Coconut Soup with Mushrooms
- Thai Cabbage Salad with Lime Dressing
- Thai Grilled Shrimp Skewers
- Thai Spicy Chicken Wings
- Thai Sweet and Sour Stir-Fry
- Thai BBQ Ribs
- Thai Coconut Rice (Khao Mamuang)

- Thai Sweet Sticky Rice with Mango
- Thai Shrimp Toast
- Thai Baked Coconut Pudding
- Thai Pineapple Curry
- Thai Grilled Eggplant Salad
- Thai Creamy Corn Soup
- Thai Rice Noodle Salad
- Thai Spicy Tamarind Sauce
- Thai Mushroom Stir-Fry
- Thai Red Lentil Curry
- Thai Fish Sauce Wings
- Thai Basil Tofu Stir-Fry
- Thai Sweet Potato Curry
- Thai Chili Lime Chicken Salad
- Thai Green Tea Ice Cream

Pad Thai

Ingredients:

- 200g rice noodles
- 150g shrimp or chicken, sliced
- 2 eggs
- 1 cup bean sprouts
- 2 tablespoons fish sauce
- 1 tablespoon tamarind paste
- 1 tablespoon sugar
- 2 tablespoons peanuts, crushed
- 2 green onions, chopped
- Lime wedges for serving
- Oil for cooking

Instructions:

1. **Prepare Noodles:**
    - Soak rice noodles in warm water for 30 minutes until soft, then drain.
2. **Cook Protein:**
    - Heat oil in a pan. Add shrimp or chicken and cook until done.
3. **Add Eggs:**
    - Push protein to one side, crack in eggs, and scramble until cooked.
4. **Combine:**
    - Add drained noodles, fish sauce, tamarind paste, and sugar. Toss until well combined.
5. **Finish:**
    - Stir in bean sprouts and green onions. Serve topped with crushed peanuts and lime wedges.

Tom Yum Goong (Spicy Shrimp Soup)

Ingredients:

- 300g shrimp, peeled and deveined
- 4 cups water
- 2 stalks lemongrass, cut into pieces
- 4-5 kaffir lime leaves
- 3-4 slices galangal
- 2-3 Thai bird's eye chilies, smashed
- 200g mushrooms, sliced
- 2 tablespoons fish sauce
- 1 tablespoon lime juice
- Fresh cilantro for garnish

Instructions:

1. **Boil Broth:**
   - In a pot, bring water to a boil. Add lemongrass, kaffir lime leaves, galangal, and chilies. Simmer for 10 minutes.
2. **Add Shrimp:**
   - Add shrimp and mushrooms. Cook until shrimp turns pink.
3. **Season:**
   - Stir in fish sauce and lime juice. Remove from heat.
4. **Serve:**
   - Garnish with fresh cilantro before serving.

Green Curry (Gaeng Keow Wan)

Ingredients:

- 400g chicken, sliced
- 2 tablespoons green curry paste
- 1 can coconut milk
- 1 cup eggplant, diced
- 1 cup bell peppers, sliced
- 1 cup Thai basil leaves
- 2 tablespoons fish sauce
- 1 tablespoon sugar
- Oil for cooking

Instructions:

1. **Cook Paste:**
    - In a pot, heat oil and fry green curry paste until fragrant.
2. **Add Chicken:**
    - Add chicken and cook until browned.
3. **Add Coconut Milk:**
    - Pour in coconut milk, then add eggplant and bell peppers. Simmer until cooked.
4. **Finish:**
    - Stir in fish sauce, sugar, and basil leaves. Serve with rice.

Massaman Curry

Ingredients:

- 500g beef or chicken, cubed
- 2 tablespoons Massaman curry paste
- 1 can coconut milk
- 2 potatoes, cubed
- 1 onion, chopped
- 1 tablespoon fish sauce
- 1 tablespoon tamarind paste
- 2 tablespoons peanuts, crushed

Instructions:

1. **Cook Paste:**
    - In a pot, heat oil and fry Massaman curry paste until fragrant.
2. **Add Meat:**
    - Add beef or chicken and cook until browned.
3. **Add Ingredients:**
    - Pour in coconut milk, then add potatoes, onion, fish sauce, and tamarind paste. Simmer until meat and potatoes are tender.
4. **Serve:**
    - Top with crushed peanuts before serving with rice.

Tom Kha Gai (Chicken Coconut Soup)

Ingredients:

- 300g chicken, sliced
- 4 cups chicken broth
- 1 can coconut milk
- 2 stalks lemongrass, cut into pieces
- 4-5 kaffir lime leaves
- 3-4 slices galangal
- 2-3 Thai bird's eye chilies, smashed
- 2 tablespoons fish sauce
- 1 tablespoon lime juice
- Fresh cilantro for garnish

Instructions:

1. **Boil Broth:**
    - In a pot, bring chicken broth to a boil. Add lemongrass, kaffir lime leaves, galangal, and chilies. Simmer for 10 minutes.
2. **Add Chicken:**
    - Add chicken slices and cook until done.
3. **Add Coconut Milk:**
    - Pour in coconut milk, then stir in fish sauce and lime juice.
4. **Serve:**
    - Garnish with fresh cilantro before serving.

Som Tum (Green Papaya Salad)

Ingredients:

- 2 cups green papaya, shredded
- 1/2 cup cherry tomatoes, halved
- 1/4 cup green beans, cut into pieces
- 2-3 Thai bird's eye chilies, smashed
- 2 tablespoons fish sauce
- 1 tablespoon lime juice
- 1 tablespoon sugar
- Crushed peanuts for garnish

Instructions:

1. **Mix Ingredients:**
    - In a bowl, combine green papaya, tomatoes, green beans, and chilies.
2. **Make Dressing:**
    - In another bowl, whisk fish sauce, lime juice, and sugar until dissolved.
3. **Combine:**
    - Pour dressing over salad and toss to combine.
4. **Serve:**
    - Garnish with crushed peanuts before serving.

Larb Gai (Spicy Chicken Salad)

Ingredients:

- 400g ground chicken
- 1/2 cup mint leaves, chopped
- 1/4 cup cilantro, chopped
- 2-3 Thai bird's eye chilies, smashed
- 2 tablespoons fish sauce
- 1 tablespoon lime juice
- 1 tablespoon toasted rice powder

Instructions:

1. **Cook Chicken:**
    - In a pan, cook ground chicken until fully cooked.
2. **Combine Ingredients:**
    - In a bowl, mix cooked chicken, mint leaves, cilantro, chilies, fish sauce, lime juice, and toasted rice powder.
3. **Serve:**
    - Serve warm or at room temperature, often with lettuce leaves for wrapping.

Pad Kra Pao (Basil Chicken)

Ingredients:

- 400g chicken, minced
- 4 cloves garlic, minced
- 2-3 Thai bird's eye chilies, smashed
- 2 tablespoons soy sauce
- 1 tablespoon fish sauce
- 1 tablespoon sugar
- 1 cup Thai basil leaves
- Oil for cooking

Instructions:

1. **Cook Chicken:**
   - In a pan, heat oil and fry garlic and chilies until fragrant.
2. **Add Chicken:**
   - Add minced chicken and cook until browned.
3. **Season:**
   - Stir in soy sauce, fish sauce, and sugar. Cook for another minute.
4. **Finish:**
   - Add basil leaves and stir until wilted. Serve with rice and fried eggs.

Pad See Ew (Stir-Fried Flat Noodles)

Ingredients:

- 200g flat rice noodles
- 150g chicken or beef, sliced
- 2 cups broccoli or Chinese broccoli
- 2 eggs
- 3 tablespoons soy sauce
- 1 tablespoon oyster sauce
- 1 tablespoon sugar
- 2 cloves garlic, minced
- Oil for cooking

Instructions:

1. **Prepare Noodles:**
   - Soak the flat rice noodles in warm water for 30 minutes until soft. Drain and set aside.
2. **Stir-Fry:**
   - Heat oil in a wok over high heat. Add minced garlic and stir-fry until fragrant.
3. **Add Protein:**
   - Add chicken or beef and cook until browned. Push to the side.
4. **Cook Eggs:**
   - Crack in eggs and scramble until cooked, then mix with the meat.
5. **Combine Noodles:**
   - Add the noodles, soy sauce, oyster sauce, and sugar. Toss everything together.
6. **Add Vegetables:**
   - Stir in broccoli and cook until tender. Serve hot.

Khao Pad (Thai Fried Rice)

Ingredients:

- 3 cups cooked jasmine rice
- 150g chicken, shrimp, or tofu, diced
- 1 cup mixed vegetables (carrots, peas, corn)
- 2 eggs
- 3 tablespoons soy sauce
- 1 tablespoon fish sauce
- 2 green onions, chopped
- Oil for cooking

Instructions:

1. **Heat Oil:**
    - In a pan, heat oil and scramble the eggs until just set. Remove and set aside.
2. **Cook Protein:**
    - In the same pan, add more oil and cook the chicken, shrimp, or tofu until done.
3. **Add Vegetables:**
    - Stir in the mixed vegetables and cook until tender.
4. **Add Rice:**
    - Add the cooked rice, soy sauce, and fish sauce. Stir-fry until well mixed.
5. **Finish:**
    - Stir in scrambled eggs and green onions. Serve with lime wedges.

Moo Pad Krapow (Stir-Fried Pork with Basil)

Ingredients:

- 400g ground pork
- 4 cloves garlic, minced
- 2-3 Thai bird's eye chilies, chopped
- 2 tablespoons soy sauce
- 1 tablespoon fish sauce
- 1 tablespoon sugar
- 1 cup Thai basil leaves
- Oil for cooking

Instructions:

1. **Heat Oil:**
   - In a pan, heat oil and sauté garlic and chilies until fragrant.
2. **Cook Pork:**
   - Add ground pork and cook until browned.
3. **Season:**
   - Stir in soy sauce, fish sauce, and sugar. Cook for another minute.
4. **Add Basil:**
   - Toss in the Thai basil leaves and stir until wilted. Serve with rice and fried eggs.

Pla Rad Prik (Crispy Fish with Chili Sauce)

Ingredients:

- 1 whole fish (e.g., tilapia), cleaned and scored
- 1/2 cup cornstarch
- Oil for frying
- 1/2 cup chili sauce
- 2 cloves garlic, minced
- 1 tablespoon fish sauce
- 1 tablespoon sugar
- Fresh cilantro for garnish

Instructions:

1. **Prepare Fish:**
   - Coat the fish with cornstarch, shaking off the excess.
2. **Fry Fish:**
   - Heat oil in a deep pan and fry the fish until golden and crispy. Drain on paper towels.
3. **Make Sauce:**
   - In another pan, heat a little oil and sauté garlic until fragrant. Add chili sauce, fish sauce, and sugar, stirring until well mixed.
4. **Serve:**
   - Place the fried fish on a plate, drizzle with sauce, and garnish with cilantro.

Gai Yang (Grilled Chicken)

Ingredients:

- 4 chicken thighs or drumsticks
- 3 tablespoons soy sauce
- 2 tablespoons fish sauce
- 2 tablespoons brown sugar
- 2 cloves garlic, minced
- 1 tablespoon black pepper
- Lime wedges for serving

Instructions:

1. **Marinate Chicken:**
    - In a bowl, combine soy sauce, fish sauce, brown sugar, garlic, and black pepper. Add chicken and marinate for at least 30 minutes.
2. **Grill Chicken:**
    - Preheat the grill and cook chicken until fully cooked and charred on the outside.
3. **Serve:**
    - Serve with lime wedges and your favorite dipping sauce.

Thai Fish Cakes (Tod Mun Pla)

Ingredients:

- 300g fish fillets (e.g., cod), minced
- 2 tablespoons red curry paste
- 1 tablespoon fish sauce
- 1 tablespoon lime juice
- 1/4 cup green beans, chopped
- Oil for frying
- Cucumber relish for serving

Instructions:

1. **Make Mixture:**
    - In a bowl, combine minced fish, curry paste, fish sauce, lime juice, and green beans. Mix well.
2. **Form Cakes:**
    - Shape the mixture into small patties.
3. **Fry Cakes:**
    - Heat oil in a pan and fry fish cakes until golden brown on both sides. Drain on paper towels.
4. **Serve:**
    - Serve with cucumber relish.

Thai Beef Salad (Yum Nua)

Ingredients:

- 300g beef, grilled and sliced
- 1 cup mixed salad greens
- 1/2 cup cherry tomatoes, halved
- 1/4 cup cucumber, sliced
- 2 tablespoons fish sauce
- 1 tablespoon lime juice
- 1 tablespoon sugar
- 2-3 Thai bird's eye chilies, sliced

Instructions:

1. **Make Dressing:**
   - In a bowl, whisk together fish sauce, lime juice, sugar, and chilies.
2. **Combine Salad:**
   - In a large bowl, mix salad greens, cherry tomatoes, cucumber, and grilled beef.
3. **Add Dressing:**
   - Pour dressing over the salad and toss gently. Serve immediately.

Khao Soi (Curry Noodle Soup)

Ingredients:

- 200g egg noodles
- 300g chicken or beef, sliced
- 1 can coconut milk
- 2 tablespoons red curry paste
- 4 cups chicken broth
- 1 tablespoon soy sauce
- 1 tablespoon fish sauce
- 1 cup pickled mustard greens
- Lime wedges for serving
- Fresh cilantro for garnish

Instructions:

1. **Cook Noodles:**
    - Boil egg noodles according to package instructions. Drain and set aside.
2. **Make Curry:**
    - In a pot, heat oil and fry red curry paste until fragrant. Add chicken and cook until browned.
3. **Add Liquids:**
    - Pour in coconut milk and chicken broth. Simmer for 15 minutes.
4. **Finish:**
    - Stir in soy sauce and fish sauce. Serve hot over noodles, topped with pickled mustard greens, cilantro, and lime wedges.

Thai Spring Rolls

Ingredients:

- 10 rice paper wrappers
- 100g vermicelli noodles, cooked
- 1 cup lettuce, shredded
- 1 carrot, julienned
- 1 cucumber, julienned
- 1 cup cooked shrimp or tofu, sliced
- Fresh mint and cilantro leaves
- Soy sauce or sweet chili sauce for dipping

Instructions:

1. **Prepare Filling:**
    - In a bowl, combine cooked vermicelli noodles, lettuce, carrot, cucumber, shrimp or tofu, mint, and cilantro.
2. **Soak Wrappers:**
    - Soak rice paper wrappers in warm water until soft.
3. **Wrap:**
    - Place a wrapper on a flat surface, add a portion of the filling, fold in the sides, and roll tightly.
4. **Serve:**
    - Serve with soy sauce or sweet chili sauce for dipping.

Thai Chili and Garlic Noodles

Ingredients:

- 200g egg noodles
- 4 cloves garlic, minced
- 2-3 Thai bird's eye chilies, chopped
- 2 tablespoons soy sauce
- 1 tablespoon oyster sauce
- 1 tablespoon sesame oil
- Fresh cilantro for garnish

Instructions:

1. **Cook Noodles:**
   - Boil the egg noodles according to package instructions. Drain and set aside.
2. **Sauté Garlic:**
   - In a pan, heat sesame oil and sauté minced garlic and chilies until fragrant.
3. **Combine:**
   - Add cooked noodles, soy sauce, and oyster sauce. Toss until well mixed.
4. **Garnish:**
   - Serve hot, garnished with fresh cilantro.

Thai Grilled Pork Skewers (Moo Ping)

Ingredients:

- 500g pork shoulder, thinly sliced
- 3 tablespoons soy sauce
- 2 tablespoons fish sauce
- 1 tablespoon sugar
- 2 cloves garlic, minced
- 1 tablespoon black pepper
- Bamboo skewers

Instructions:

1. **Marinate Pork:**
    - In a bowl, combine soy sauce, fish sauce, sugar, garlic, and black pepper. Add pork and marinate for at least 30 minutes.
2. **Skewer:**
    - Thread marinated pork onto bamboo skewers.
3. **Grill:**
    - Preheat the grill and cook skewers for about 10-15 minutes, turning occasionally until cooked through.
4. **Serve:**
    - Serve with sweet chili sauce.

Green Mango Salad

Ingredients:

- 1 green mango, julienned
- 1 carrot, julienned
- 1/2 cup red bell pepper, sliced
- 1/4 cup roasted peanuts, crushed
- 2 tablespoons fish sauce
- 1 tablespoon lime juice
- 1 tablespoon sugar
- Fresh cilantro for garnish

Instructions:

1. **Make Dressing:**
   - In a bowl, whisk together fish sauce, lime juice, and sugar.
2. **Combine Salad:**
   - In a large bowl, mix julienned mango, carrot, bell pepper, and dressing.
3. **Garnish:**
   - Top with crushed peanuts and fresh cilantro. Serve immediately.

Thai Fried Tofu with Peanut Sauce

Ingredients:

- 300g firm tofu, cubed
- Oil for frying
- 1/4 cup peanut butter
- 2 tablespoons soy sauce
- 1 tablespoon lime juice
- 1 tablespoon honey or sugar
- Water for thinning

Instructions:

1. **Fry Tofu:**
    - Heat oil in a pan and fry tofu cubes until golden brown. Drain on paper towels.
2. **Make Sauce:**
    - In a bowl, whisk together peanut butter, soy sauce, lime juice, honey, and enough water to achieve desired consistency.
3. **Serve:**
    - Serve fried tofu drizzled with peanut sauce.

Pad Woon Sen (Stir-Fried Glass Noodles)

Ingredients:

- 200g glass noodles, soaked in warm water
- 150g chicken, shrimp, or tofu, sliced
- 1 cup mixed vegetables (carrots, bell peppers, broccoli)
- 2 eggs, beaten
- 2 tablespoons soy sauce
- 1 tablespoon oyster sauce
- 1 tablespoon sugar
- Oil for cooking

Instructions:

1. **Cook Protein:**
   - In a pan, heat oil and stir-fry chicken, shrimp, or tofu until cooked through.
2. **Add Vegetables:**
   - Stir in mixed vegetables and cook until tender.
3. **Add Noodles:**
   - Add soaked glass noodles, soy sauce, oyster sauce, and sugar. Toss well.
4. **Finish:**
   - Push noodles to one side, add beaten eggs, and scramble. Mix everything together and serve hot.

Thai Pineapple Fried Rice

Ingredients:

- 3 cups cooked jasmine rice
- 1 cup pineapple chunks
- 150g chicken, shrimp, or tofu, diced
- 1/2 cup peas and carrots
- 2 eggs
- 3 tablespoons soy sauce
- 1 tablespoon fish sauce
- 1/2 teaspoon curry powder
- Oil for cooking

Instructions:

1. **Heat Oil:**
   - In a pan, heat oil and scramble eggs until just set. Remove and set aside.
2. **Cook Protein:**
   - In the same pan, add more oil and cook the chicken, shrimp, or tofu until done.
3. **Add Vegetables:**
   - Stir in pineapple, peas, and carrots. Cook for a few minutes.
4. **Add Rice:**
   - Add cooked rice, soy sauce, fish sauce, and curry powder. Stir-fry until well combined.
5. **Finish:**
   - Stir in scrambled eggs and serve hot.

Thai Vegetable Stir-Fry (Pad Pak Ruam Mit)

Ingredients:

- 2 cups mixed vegetables (broccoli, bell peppers, carrots)
- 2 cloves garlic, minced
- 2 tablespoons soy sauce
- 1 tablespoon oyster sauce
- 1 tablespoon sugar
- Oil for cooking

Instructions:

1. **Heat Oil:**
   - In a pan, heat oil and sauté minced garlic until fragrant.
2. **Add Vegetables:**
   - Add mixed vegetables and stir-fry for about 3-4 minutes.
3. **Season:**
   - Add soy sauce, oyster sauce, and sugar. Cook for another minute.
4. **Serve:**
   - Serve hot as a side dish or over rice.

Spicy Glass Noodle Salad (Yum Woon Sen)

Ingredients:

- 200g glass noodles, soaked and drained
- 150g cooked shrimp or chicken
- 1/2 cup cherry tomatoes, halved
- 1/4 cup red onion, thinly sliced
- 2-3 Thai bird's eye chilies, chopped
- 3 tablespoons fish sauce
- 2 tablespoons lime juice
- Fresh cilantro for garnish

Instructions:

1. **Combine Ingredients:**
   - In a large bowl, mix glass noodles, shrimp or chicken, cherry tomatoes, red onion, and chilies.
2. **Make Dressing:**
   - In a separate bowl, whisk together fish sauce and lime juice. Pour over the salad and toss to combine.
3. **Garnish:**
   - Serve garnished with fresh cilantro.

Thai Garlic Pepper Chicken

Ingredients:

- 500g chicken thighs, boneless and skinless, sliced
- 5 cloves garlic, minced
- 1 teaspoon black pepper
- 2 tablespoons soy sauce
- 2 tablespoons oyster sauce
- 1 tablespoon sugar
- 1 tablespoon vegetable oil
- Green onions for garnish

Instructions:

1. **Marinate Chicken:**
    - In a bowl, mix chicken, garlic, black pepper, soy sauce, oyster sauce, and sugar. Marinate for at least 30 minutes.
2. **Heat Oil:**
    - In a large pan, heat vegetable oil over medium-high heat.
3. **Cook Chicken:**
    - Add marinated chicken and stir-fry until cooked through and slightly caramelized, about 5-7 minutes.
4. **Garnish:**
    - Serve hot, garnished with sliced green onions.

Thai Red Curry with Duck

Ingredients:

- 500g duck breast, sliced
- 2 tablespoons red curry paste
- 400ml coconut milk
- 1 cup mixed vegetables (bell peppers, bamboo shoots, Thai basil)
- 1 tablespoon fish sauce
- 1 tablespoon sugar
- Fresh basil for garnish

Instructions:

1. **Cook Duck:**
   - In a pan, cook duck slices until browned and cooked through. Remove and set aside.
2. **Make Curry:**
   - In the same pan, add red curry paste and fry for 1-2 minutes. Stir in coconut milk and bring to a simmer.
3. **Add Vegetables:**
   - Add mixed vegetables, fish sauce, and sugar. Cook for 5 minutes.
4. **Combine:**
   - Return duck to the pan and simmer for an additional 5 minutes.
5. **Garnish:**
   - Serve hot, garnished with fresh basil.

Thai Spicy Seafood Salad (Yum Talay)

Ingredients:

- 200g shrimp, peeled and deveined
- 200g squid, sliced
- 100g fish fillet, cubed
- 1/2 cup cherry tomatoes, halved
- 1/4 cup red onion, thinly sliced
- 2-3 Thai bird's eye chilies, chopped
- 3 tablespoons fish sauce
- 2 tablespoons lime juice
- Fresh cilantro for garnish

Instructions:

1. **Cook Seafood:**
   - Boil shrimp, squid, and fish until cooked. Drain and set aside.
2. **Combine Salad:**
   - In a bowl, mix cooked seafood, cherry tomatoes, red onion, and chilies.
3. **Make Dressing:**
   - In a separate bowl, whisk together fish sauce and lime juice. Pour over the salad and toss to combine.
4. **Garnish:**
   - Serve garnished with fresh cilantro.

Thai Coconut Soup with Mushrooms

Ingredients:

- 400ml coconut milk
- 2 cups vegetable or chicken broth
- 200g mushrooms, sliced
- 1 stalk lemongrass, smashed
- 3-4 kaffir lime leaves
- 2-3 Thai bird's eye chilies
- 2 tablespoons fish sauce
- 1 tablespoon lime juice
- Fresh cilantro for garnish

Instructions:

1. **Simmer Broth:**
   - In a pot, combine coconut milk, broth, lemongrass, kaffir lime leaves, and chilies. Simmer for 10 minutes.
2. **Add Mushrooms:**
   - Add mushrooms and cook until tender.
3. **Season:**
   - Stir in fish sauce and lime juice. Simmer for another 5 minutes.
4. **Garnish:**
   - Serve hot, garnished with fresh cilantro.

Thai Cabbage Salad with Lime Dressing

Ingredients:

- 4 cups green cabbage, shredded
- 1 carrot, shredded
- 1/4 cup red onion, thinly sliced
- 1/4 cup roasted peanuts, crushed
- 2 tablespoons lime juice
- 1 tablespoon fish sauce
- 1 tablespoon sugar
- Fresh cilantro for garnish

Instructions:

1. **Make Dressing:**
    - In a bowl, whisk together lime juice, fish sauce, and sugar.
2. **Combine Salad:**
    - In a large bowl, mix shredded cabbage, carrot, red onion, and dressing.
3. **Garnish:**
    - Top with crushed peanuts and fresh cilantro. Serve immediately.

Thai Grilled Shrimp Skewers

Ingredients:

- 500g shrimp, peeled and deveined
- 2 tablespoons fish sauce
- 1 tablespoon soy sauce
- 1 tablespoon sugar
- 2 cloves garlic, minced
- Bamboo skewers

Instructions:

1. **Marinate Shrimp:**
    - In a bowl, combine shrimp, fish sauce, soy sauce, sugar, and garlic. Marinate for at least 30 minutes.
2. **Skewer:**
    - Thread marinated shrimp onto bamboo skewers.
3. **Grill:**
    - Preheat the grill and cook skewers for about 3-4 minutes on each side until shrimp are cooked.
4. **Serve:**
    - Serve with a side of sweet chili sauce.

Thai Spicy Chicken Wings

Ingredients:

- 1kg chicken wings
- 3 tablespoons fish sauce
- 2 tablespoons soy sauce
- 2 tablespoons brown sugar
- 1 tablespoon lime juice
- 2-3 Thai bird's eye chilies, chopped
- Oil for frying

Instructions:

1. **Marinate Wings:**
   - In a bowl, mix chicken wings with fish sauce, soy sauce, brown sugar, lime juice, and chilies. Marinate for at least 1 hour.
2. **Heat Oil:**
   - In a deep pan, heat oil for frying.
3. **Fry Wings:**
   - Fry marinated wings until golden brown and cooked through, about 10-12 minutes.
4. **Serve:**
   - Serve hot with lime wedges.

Thai Sweet and Sour Stir-Fry

Ingredients:

- 500g chicken or tofu, diced
- 1 cup bell peppers, chopped
- 1 cup pineapple chunks
- 1 onion, sliced
- 2-3 cloves garlic, minced
- 3 tablespoons ketchup
- 2 tablespoons soy sauce
- 1 tablespoon vinegar
- 1 tablespoon sugar
- Oil for cooking

Instructions:

1. **Heat Oil:**
   - In a pan, heat oil and sauté garlic and onion until fragrant.
2. **Add Chicken/Tofu:**
   - Add diced chicken or tofu and cook until browned.
3. **Add Vegetables:**
   - Stir in bell peppers, pineapple, ketchup, soy sauce, vinegar, and sugar. Cook until vegetables are tender.
4. **Serve:**
   - Serve hot over rice.

Thai BBQ Ribs

Ingredients:

- 1 kg pork ribs
- 3 tablespoons soy sauce
- 3 tablespoons fish sauce
- 3 tablespoons brown sugar
- 2 tablespoons honey
- 2 tablespoons tamarind paste
- 2-3 cloves garlic, minced
- 1 tablespoon black pepper
- Sesame seeds for garnish

Instructions:

1. **Prepare Marinade:**
   - In a bowl, combine soy sauce, fish sauce, brown sugar, honey, tamarind paste, garlic, and black pepper. Mix well.
2. **Marinate Ribs:**
   - Place ribs in a large resealable bag and pour marinade over them. Seal and refrigerate for at least 2 hours or overnight.
3. **Preheat Oven:**
   - Preheat your oven to 150°C (300°F). Line a baking tray with foil.
4. **Bake Ribs:**
   - Remove ribs from marinade and place them on the baking tray. Bake for 2-3 hours, basting occasionally with remaining marinade.
5. **Grill Ribs:**
   - Preheat a grill or BBQ. Grill ribs for about 5-10 minutes until caramelized and slightly charred.
6. **Garnish:**
   - Serve hot, garnished with sesame seeds.

Thai Coconut Rice (Khao Mamuang)

Ingredients:

- 2 cups jasmine rice
- 1 can (400ml) coconut milk
- 1 cup water
- 1 tablespoon sugar
- 1/2 teaspoon salt
- 1/4 cup shredded coconut (optional)

Instructions:

1. **Rinse Rice:**
   - Rinse jasmine rice under cold water until water runs clear.
2. **Combine Ingredients:**
   - In a pot, combine rice, coconut milk, water, sugar, and salt. Stir to mix.
3. **Cook Rice:**
   - Bring to a boil, then reduce heat to low. Cover and simmer for about 15-20 minutes until rice is cooked and liquid is absorbed.
4. **Fluff Rice:**
   - Remove from heat and let it sit covered for 10 minutes. Fluff with a fork and stir in shredded coconut if using.
5. **Serve:**
   - Serve warm as a side dish or dessert.

Thai Sweet Sticky Rice with Mango

Ingredients:

- 1 cup glutinous rice
- 1 can (400ml) coconut milk
- 1/2 cup sugar
- 1/4 teaspoon salt
- 2 ripe mangoes, peeled and sliced
- Sesame seeds or mung beans for garnish

Instructions:

1. **Soak Rice:**
    - Soak glutinous rice in water for at least 4 hours or overnight. Drain.
2. **Steam Rice:**
    - Steam rice in a bamboo or metal steamer lined with cheesecloth for about 20-30 minutes until cooked.
3. **Prepare Coconut Sauce:**
    - In a saucepan, heat coconut milk, sugar, and salt until dissolved. Reserve a small amount for drizzling.
4. **Combine Rice and Sauce:**
    - In a bowl, combine steamed rice with the coconut sauce and mix well. Let it sit for about 30 minutes.
5. **Serve:**
    - Serve sticky rice topped with sliced mango and drizzled with reserved coconut sauce. Garnish with sesame seeds or mung beans.

Thai Shrimp Toast

Ingredients:

- 200g shrimp, peeled and deveined
- 2 slices white bread, crusts removed
- 1 egg
- 1 tablespoon fish sauce
- 2-3 cloves garlic, minced
- 1 teaspoon white pepper
- Oil for frying
- Sesame seeds for garnish

Instructions:

1. **Prepare Shrimp Mixture:**
   - In a food processor, combine shrimp, egg, fish sauce, garlic, and white pepper. Blend until smooth.
2. **Spread on Bread:**
   - Spread the shrimp mixture evenly over each slice of bread. Cut each slice into quarters.
3. **Heat Oil:**
   - In a frying pan, heat oil over medium heat.
4. **Fry Toast:**
   - Fry the shrimp toast, shrimp side down, until golden brown and crispy, about 3-4 minutes per side.
5. **Garnish:**
   - Serve hot, garnished with sesame seeds.

Thai Baked Coconut Pudding

Ingredients:

- 1 cup coconut milk
- 1/2 cup sugar
- 1/2 cup rice flour
- 1/4 teaspoon salt
- 2 eggs
- 1 teaspoon vanilla extract
- Fresh coconut or pandan leaves for garnish (optional)

Instructions:

1. **Preheat Oven:**
    - Preheat your oven to 175°C (350°F).
2. **Mix Ingredients:**
    - In a bowl, whisk together coconut milk, sugar, rice flour, salt, eggs, and vanilla until smooth.
3. **Pour into Baking Dish:**
    - Pour the mixture into a greased baking dish.
4. **Bake:**
    - Bake for 25-30 minutes or until the top is golden and a toothpick comes out clean.
5. **Serve:**
    - Allow to cool, then cut into squares and serve, garnished with fresh coconut or pandan leaves if desired.

Thai Pineapple Curry

Ingredients:

- 500g chicken or tofu, diced
- 1 cup pineapple chunks
- 1 cup coconut milk
- 2 tablespoons red curry paste
- 1 tablespoon fish sauce
- 1 tablespoon sugar
- 1 red bell pepper, sliced
- Fresh basil for garnish

Instructions:

1. **Cook Chicken/Tofu:**
   - In a pot, heat oil and cook chicken or tofu until browned.
2. **Add Curry Paste:**
   - Stir in red curry paste and cook for 1-2 minutes until fragrant.
3. **Add Coconut Milk:**
   - Pour in coconut milk, fish sauce, sugar, and pineapple chunks. Simmer for about 10 minutes.
4. **Add Bell Pepper:**
   - Add bell pepper and cook for an additional 5 minutes.
5. **Garnish:**
   - Serve hot, garnished with fresh basil.

Thai Grilled Eggplant Salad

Ingredients:

- 2 medium eggplants, sliced
- 1/2 cup cherry tomatoes, halved
- 1/4 cup red onion, sliced
- 2-3 Thai bird's eye chilies, chopped
- 2 tablespoons fish sauce
- 2 tablespoons lime juice
- 1 tablespoon sugar
- Fresh cilantro for garnish

Instructions:

1. **Grill Eggplant:**
   - Preheat the grill and grill eggplant slices until charred and tender. Set aside to cool.
2. **Prepare Dressing:**
   - In a bowl, mix fish sauce, lime juice, and sugar until dissolved.
3. **Combine Salad:**
   - In a large bowl, combine grilled eggplant, cherry tomatoes, red onion, and chilies. Pour dressing over and toss to combine.
4. **Garnish:**
   - Serve at room temperature, garnished with fresh cilantro.

Thai Creamy Corn Soup

Ingredients:

- 2 cups corn kernels (fresh or frozen)
- 400ml coconut milk
- 2 cups vegetable broth
- 1 onion, chopped
- 2-3 cloves garlic, minced
- 1 tablespoon sugar
- Salt and pepper to taste
- Fresh cilantro for garnish

Instructions:

1. **Sauté Vegetables:**
   - In a pot, heat oil and sauté onion and garlic until translucent.
2. **Add Corn:**
   - Stir in corn and cook for 5 minutes.
3. **Add Liquids:**
   - Pour in coconut milk and vegetable broth. Bring to a boil, then simmer for 10-15 minutes.
4. **Blend Soup:**
   - Use an immersion blender to puree the soup until smooth. Season with sugar, salt, and pepper.
5. **Serve:**
   - Serve hot, garnished with fresh cilantro.

Thai Rice Noodle Salad

Ingredients:

- 200g rice noodles
- 1 cup mixed vegetables (carrots, bell peppers, cucumbers, shredded cabbage)
- 1/4 cup chopped cilantro
- 1/4 cup chopped peanuts
- 2 tablespoons lime juice
- 2 tablespoons fish sauce
- 1 tablespoon sugar
- 1 tablespoon soy sauce
- 1 teaspoon chili flakes (optional)

Instructions:

1. **Cook Noodles:**
    - Cook rice noodles according to package instructions. Drain and rinse with cold water.
2. **Prepare Dressing:**
    - In a bowl, whisk together lime juice, fish sauce, sugar, soy sauce, and chili flakes.
3. **Combine Ingredients:**
    - In a large bowl, combine noodles, mixed vegetables, and cilantro. Pour dressing over and toss to combine.
4. **Serve:**
    - Serve chilled or at room temperature, garnished with chopped peanuts.

Thai Spicy Tamarind Sauce

Ingredients:

- 1/4 cup tamarind paste
- 2 tablespoons sugar
- 2 tablespoons fish sauce
- 1 tablespoon soy sauce
- 1 tablespoon lime juice
- 1-2 Thai bird's eye chilies, minced
- Water as needed

Instructions:

1. **Mix Ingredients:**
   - In a bowl, combine tamarind paste, sugar, fish sauce, soy sauce, lime juice, and minced chilies.
2. **Adjust Consistency:**
   - Add water to thin the sauce to your desired consistency. Mix well.
3. **Serve:**
   - Use as a dipping sauce or drizzle over dishes as desired.

Thai Mushroom Stir-Fry

Ingredients:

- 300g mushrooms (shiitake, oyster, or button), sliced
- 2 tablespoons soy sauce
- 1 tablespoon oyster sauce (optional)
- 2-3 cloves garlic, minced
- 1 tablespoon vegetable oil
- 1 cup mixed vegetables (bell peppers, broccoli, carrots)
- Fresh basil for garnish

Instructions:

1. **Heat Oil:**
   - In a large pan, heat vegetable oil over medium heat.
2. **Sauté Garlic:**
   - Add minced garlic and sauté for 30 seconds until fragrant.
3. **Add Mushrooms:**
   - Add sliced mushrooms and cook until browned.
4. **Add Vegetables:**
   - Add mixed vegetables and stir-fry for another 3-5 minutes.
5. **Add Sauces:**
   - Stir in soy sauce and oyster sauce. Cook for an additional 1-2 minutes.
6. **Garnish:**
   - Serve hot, garnished with fresh basil.

Thai Red Lentil Curry

Ingredients:

- 1 cup red lentils, rinsed
- 1 can (400ml) coconut milk
- 1 tablespoon red curry paste
- 2 cups vegetable broth
- 1 onion, chopped
- 2-3 cloves garlic, minced
- 1 tablespoon ginger, grated
- Salt to taste
- Fresh cilantro for garnish

Instructions:

1. **Sauté Aromatics:**
    - In a pot, heat oil and sauté onion, garlic, and ginger until translucent.
2. **Add Lentils:**
    - Stir in red lentils and red curry paste, cooking for 1-2 minutes.
3. **Add Liquids:**
    - Pour in coconut milk and vegetable broth. Bring to a boil.
4. **Simmer:**
    - Reduce heat and simmer for about 20-25 minutes until lentils are tender. Season with salt.
5. **Garnish:**
    - Serve hot, garnished with fresh cilantro.

Thai Fish Sauce Wings

Ingredients:

- 1 kg chicken wings
- 1/4 cup fish sauce
- 2 tablespoons soy sauce
- 2 tablespoons brown sugar
- 3-4 cloves garlic, minced
- 1 tablespoon lime juice
- Fresh cilantro for garnish

Instructions:

1. **Marinate Wings:**
   - In a bowl, combine fish sauce, soy sauce, brown sugar, garlic, and lime juice. Add wings and marinate for at least 1 hour.
2. **Preheat Oven:**
   - Preheat your oven to 200°C (400°F).
3. **Bake Wings:**
   - Place wings on a baking tray lined with foil. Bake for 30-40 minutes, flipping halfway, until crispy.
4. **Garnish:**
   - Serve hot, garnished with fresh cilantro.

Thai Basil Tofu Stir-Fry

Ingredients:

- 400g firm tofu, cubed
- 2 cups fresh basil leaves
- 2 tablespoons soy sauce
- 1 tablespoon oyster sauce (optional)
- 2-3 cloves garlic, minced
- 1 tablespoon vegetable oil
- 1 bell pepper, sliced
- 1 onion, sliced

Instructions:

1. **Cook Tofu:**
   - In a pan, heat oil and fry tofu cubes until golden brown. Remove and set aside.
2. **Sauté Vegetables:**
   - In the same pan, sauté garlic, onion, and bell pepper until tender.
3. **Combine Ingredients:**
   - Add tofu back to the pan, then stir in soy sauce and oyster sauce. Cook for another 2-3 minutes.
4. **Add Basil:**
   - Stir in fresh basil leaves until wilted.
5. **Serve:**
   - Serve hot with rice or noodles.

Thai Sweet Potato Curry

Ingredients:

- 1 large sweet potato, cubed
- 1 can (400ml) coconut milk
- 1 tablespoon red curry paste
- 1 cup vegetable broth
- 1 onion, chopped
- 2-3 cloves garlic, minced
- 1 tablespoon fish sauce
- Fresh cilantro for garnish

Instructions:

1. **Sauté Aromatics:**
   - In a pot, heat oil and sauté onion and garlic until translucent.
2. **Add Sweet Potato:**
   - Stir in sweet potato cubes and cook for 3-5 minutes.
3. **Add Liquids:**
   - Pour in coconut milk, vegetable broth, and red curry paste. Bring to a boil.
4. **Simmer:**
   - Reduce heat and simmer for about 20 minutes until sweet potatoes are tender. Stir in fish sauce.
5. **Garnish:**
   - Serve hot, garnished with fresh cilantro.

Thai Chili Lime Chicken Salad

Ingredients:

- 500g cooked chicken, shredded
- 1 cup mixed salad greens
- 1/2 cup cherry tomatoes, halved
- 1/2 cucumber, sliced
- 1/4 cup chopped cilantro
- 2 tablespoons lime juice
- 1 tablespoon fish sauce
- 1 tablespoon sugar
- 1 teaspoon chili flakes

Instructions:

1. **Prepare Dressing:**
   - In a bowl, mix lime juice, fish sauce, sugar, and chili flakes.
2. **Combine Salad:**
   - In a large bowl, combine shredded chicken, salad greens, cherry tomatoes, cucumber, and cilantro.
3. **Dress Salad:**
   - Drizzle dressing over the salad and toss to combine.
4. **Serve:**
   - Serve immediately.

Thai Green Tea Ice Cream

Ingredients:

- 2 cups heavy cream
- 1 cup milk
- 3/4 cup sugar
- 1/4 cup green tea powder (matcha)
- 1 teaspoon vanilla extract
- Pinch of salt

Instructions:

1. **Heat Mixture:**
    - In a saucepan, heat milk and cream over medium heat. Do not boil.
2. **Whisk in Sugar and Matcha:**
    - In a bowl, whisk together sugar, green tea powder, and salt. Gradually add hot milk mixture while whisking until smooth.
3. **Chill Mixture:**
    - Remove from heat and stir in vanilla extract. Chill the mixture in the refrigerator for at least 2 hours.
4. **Churn Ice Cream:**
    - Pour chilled mixture into an ice cream maker and churn according to manufacturer's instructions.
5. **Freeze:**
    - Transfer to a container and freeze for at least 4 hours before serving.

www.ingramcontent.com/pod-product-compliance
Lightning Source LLC
LaVergne TN
LVHW081331060526
838201LV00055B/2574